I Shouldn't Be Telling You This

Mae Leonard

𝄞 DOGHOUSE

I Shouldn't Be Telling You This

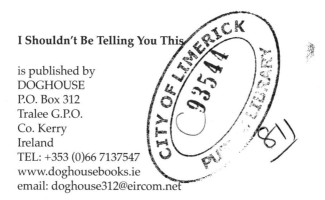

is published by
DOGHOUSE
P.O. Box 312
Tralee G.P.O.
Co. Kerry
Ireland
TEL: +353 (0)66 7137547
www.doghousebooks.ie
email: doghouse312@eircom.net

© Mae Leonard, May 2011

ISBN 978-0-9565280-4-9

Edited for DOGHOUSE by Noel King

Cover illustration: *I Shouldn't Be Telling You This* - by Ide
Leonard

The publisher and poet thank Kildare County Council
and the Educational Building Society (EBS) for their
financial support towards this publication.

Further copies available at €12, postage free, from the above
address, cheques etc. payable to DOGHOUSE also PAYPAL -
www.paypal.com to
doghousepaypal@eircom.net

Doghouse is a non-profit taking company, aiming to publish
the best of literary works by Irish or Irish resident writers.
Donations are welcome and will be acknowledged on this page.
For our 2011 publications, many thanks to

Kerry Education Service

Printed by Tralee Printing Works, Monavally, Tralee, Co. Kerry

For Joe, Ide, Una and Brian – my inspiration

Acknowledgements are due to the editors of the following where some of these poems, or versions of them, have been published or broadcast:

Six for Gold; 1995 Poets of the Year; The Great Book of Maynooth; The Kildare Anthology;
A History of Naas Hospital; The Gay Byrne Show (RTE Radio One); The Works.

Special thanks to

Noel King, for his meticulous editing and belief in me.

Contents

The Question Hung Between Us like a Poised Arrow

Who do you think you are?

   Who do I think I am?

a swan slicing a smooth lake,
the queen of Sheba on a good day,
Olga Korbut balancing on a beam,
my mother in the mirror,
my daughter when she's happy,
Marlene Dietrich craving to be alone,
Mae West at her most outrageous,
Twiggy – even at her age,
our dog sprawled on the couch,
Cinderella when she's out and about,
Mel Gibson's masseuse,
not to mention Robert Redford's dresser
and the glorious Maria Callas, bless her.

   Who do *you* think *you* are?

Progress

I shock myself sometimes,
struggling home laden
from the supermarket,
polythene handles biting
the creases of my hands
and I ask myself –
what's all this about
Women's Liberation?

I am my great grandmother
coming up the boreen
from the well, weighted
down with water buckets.

To think
I felt sorry for her
every time I turned on a tap
or flicked a switch.

Well woman?
Well now, polythene-bag woman?

Well, well, well.

Photograph

Depending on the light
and the time of year,
sun sometimes glints
the red in your hair.

I hear you chuckle
the way you used to,
knowing what I had to say.

But nobody, not even you,
could have predicted
today.

The snow avalanched,
cutting off the narrow pass
and there was no Spring.

I smile at you there
standing on the sideboard,
talk to you.

Mother

My mother's hands have developed
knobs of pain on her knuckles
and perhaps her knees or toes.
Who knows?
I never see those extremities,
hardly ever did.
I can only see the slowing down
and her dowager's hump.

A little slipping into a carelessness
in dress and cleanliness,
a dribble,
a splash of grime,
the touch of rheum in her eye
magnified by the strength
of her most recent lenses.

And she nods off at the drop of a hat,
silently, quietly, peacefully,
even during her favourite Soap.
I wonder if this is how
the end will be?

Child in a Hospital Cot

Hungry for company,
she whines all day
like a beached mermaid,
a persistent siren
that sings into my soul.

Vase

Forsaking all others, I chose you,
a stranger in my kitchen,
telling a Taiwan girl's tale
of long days dotting daises on baubles
to occidental taste.

In your slender form,
I see her struggling home
through teeming streets
where vendors sing-song enticements
to prise the few yen from her purse.

She counts her coins
and weighs just enough
for a meagre meal,
paying with her portion
of my euro.

Outside my shopping centre
a woman rattles a box
under my nose
for some Third World charity;
a euro buys me a paper circle
to stick on my lapel.

I took you home, Vase,
to fill you full of roses.

Famine Sculpture

Mould me in your mind
from the ground you stand upon,
you who never knew me;
cast me in bronze,
cast not your eyes away.
Remember me today
and tomorrow,
for all the days I hungered
and there was no one
to say a prayer or shed a tear
when they threw me here
under your feet.

Via Dolorosa

Weep not for me, O women of Jerusalem,
but for yourselves and for your children
Luke 23:28

She comes forth from the crowd,
deep concern etched on her face,
braving the awesome danger
of publicly declaring
allegiance.

Veronica.

On the roadside
amidst an hysterical mob
she alone reaches out
a supporting hand,
lifting the veil
from her face
she wipes away the blood
and is rewarded
with His image.

Veronica Guerin 1956–1996

Mary Jo

Unable to cope
with the scandalous conviction
of her son,
Mary Joe –
seventy –
weighted with trouble,
walked out
into the flooded river
above Hell's Gates
where rapids test
accomplished boatmen.

She hadn't a chance.

Don't stop me, she flung
at stunned bystanders.

Someone threw a lifebuoy.

It sashayed past her,
caught the current
and crashed against
the centre column
of Mathew Bridge.

She followed
to join the Shannon
at Curragower.

Changeable

I see
through
my kitchen window
this humdrum Monday,
dark clouds
threatening
from the East.

I have
the hearth swept,
cold ashes in the bin,
beds made,
dishes abandoned
in the sink.

A sudden squall
shivers the window pane,
prompting me
to bring in the washing.
I rush towards the door
just as the postman
shoves a hurricane
through my letterbox.

A Curragh Wren

I am a Curragh wren
flocking to the uniformed men
on the broad plains of Kildare,
a *Sile-na-Gig* with no shame.
I scoop out with my fingernail spade
a shallow nest in the brown dirt.

Is leór don dreóilin a nead.

The furze blooms a yellow birdflower
to mock my plight.
Its spiked scrub is my protection
against all weathers and whatever
the wind blows in;
all for the love of a soldier.

Is leór don dreóilin a nead.

I am a Jenny Wren,
nesting between prickly stems,
singing my love songs
in reply to his illicit mating call;
for he has a wife in other parts
serving sweet cake on porcelain plates,
whilst I await the crumbs
she casts from her table.

* *Sile-na-Gig - ancient fertility symbol.*

* *Is leór don dreóilin a nead:* old Irish saying, *the wren's nest is sufficient for its needs*

Joyce

That night
there was a sliver of new moon,
little or no light,
a threat of snow
sharpening the breeze
sweeping across The Plains.

Clumps of spiked furze
cast sinister shadows on the Curragh
when this thief came
and cut the throbbing heart out
from a Kildare home.

The expected snow fell,
covered and cleansed,
until the sun came out
on St Brigid's Day
to touch the furze with gold.

Joyce Quinn – 1952-1996

The Plains: another name for The Curragh in County Kildare.

Winter Wasp

He staggers out from a curtain fold,
this decrepit, greying old man
in a Young Munster jersey
and crawls onto our flowered wallpaper
testing a touchdown.

Passion Sunday

The priest in purple
delivering passages
of scripture
dripping with blood;
your thigh warm
against mine
on the hard pew
in the middle aisle.

Stonecrop

The broad Shannon sparkled
on the crossing from Tarbert.
Farther out the coast at Kilkee,
along by the Diamond Rocks,
stonecrop spilled its tiny pink stars
along the rising pathway.

A gardener's temptation
got the better of me,
I pulled a root.

Despite my careful nurturing,
I was positive it had died
but today in an unkempt corner
of my garden it opened
its shell pink stars
and took me back
to the crashing waves of County Clare.

Mass Path

In bare feet,
  they wore threadbare
    a line in the grasscarpet

along the Quaker hedge
  near the Mill at Ballytore
    and they continued

walking the earth
  with a dogged determination
    to cross over seven fields in allweathers

on Sunday and Holyday
  with the Griese stream
    chuckling alongside them.

Those whose land they trod
  smiled tolerantly
    behind bighouse windows

whilst donning sombre suits
  to drive the road
    to the Meeting House.

And no one called halt
  to the Massgoers trespass
    or contested their ancient right of way.

I Shouldn't Be Telling You This

I met Billy Brown today
– remember him with Derek Deane
and the Freshmen? –
and he said to me, he did,
yes, he halted and put his arm
around my shoulders
and said, *I heard you
on the radio, I did.*

And suddenly I was afraid.
Afraid that I would giggle
like the skittish schoolgirl I was
when I google-eyed at him
in his fringed, suede jacket,
his golden curls beating time
on his shoulders, as he pounded
a piano and I swung
away from Butch Moore
and the Capitol, I did.
Never liked Brendan Boyer,
and Dickie Rock was for Dubs.

Thirty years on and both of us
a little worse for wear,
yet the old spark was there
as I walked down the aisle with him
in the supermarket today;
but I gave my wedding dress away.

The Man from Labasheeda

The waves of Clonderlaw Bay
in his hair, he extends his hand
requesting me to dance
in that old-fashioned way,
the lights of Killimer
spotlighting his slight bow,
quizzing of eyebrow,
and serious eye to eye,
until my nod cracks a smile
on his honest West Clare face.

He leads me a merry dance
gliding on practised sails.
I follow awkwardly
until, close together,
we get it altogether
around the tiny dance floor.
Encouraged by the romance
of a smooth Atlantic Ocean
and the sultry summer night,
he whispers huskily in my ear –

Jays, if I got you into my bed,
I wouldn't let you out for a year!

Going with Domingo

Neither here nor there,
Placido and I
doing ninety, somewhere
between Limerick and Naas.

A single magpie flashes
at Roscrea. Bah!
What does he know
of our secret affaire?

Home to Our Mountains,
swings me back
several years
to the school operetta.

Eyes fixed on the road,
I conduct the air above
the steering wheel,
loving the power of *Granada*.

After Monasterevin
a juggernaught challenges.
Should I?
Placido says – No! No!
so I tuck us in behind it
duetting *O Paradis*.

Dein Ist Mein Ganzes Herz,
takes us to the Newbridge bypass
where I turn off for Naas.

Garda Síochána in my Parlour

I cannot look at that chair again
but see his silverbuttoned,
blue uniformed self-telling – nightmare.

Even now, the feeling persists
drying my mouth, robbing my voice
and goosepimpling my skin – horror.

A fearful buzzing deafened my ears,
blotting out the message
but the aftershock was seismic.

In the ensuing silence
the grandmother clock on the wall
ticked with anvil strength

and the fire danced
like a clown at a funeral,
while my legs numbed to the knees.

Man–of–War

On my breakfast table
a crimsoned corpse,
a spectre in jeans, combat jacket
and trendy army boots,
lying on a rain-drenched street
of some warracked city,
arms splayed, fingers painclenched
surrounded by coldeyed men.

This picture of a boy in full colour
emblazoned on the front page
of my morning newspaper,
some mother's son
and no one there to mourn him,
only curious furhatted strangers
with emotionless hungry faces
encircling his bloody corpse.

This, once a boy in jeans,
combat jacket and trendy army boots,
lies on the concrete street.
I turn it over
and pour out my coffee.

The Woman's Rath *

O Great Daghda* take this woman,
our most precious possession –
perfect, beautiful, pure, a fertile virgin,
earth to earth she is our gift
to satisfy your great hunger.

We have her prepared,
anointed her body with perfumed oils,
coiled her hair, dressed her
in our best bleached-flax wedding garment,
strung amber beads around her neck
to pleasure you.

No! Heed not her scream,
she comes to you in high ecstasy,
her mouth wide open ready to do your will,
and when she does, pray grant us
the rain you are holding
so that our crops will thrive,
so that we can eat,
so that we can laugh,
so that we can make love
to make more beautiful virgins
should you have hunger for them.

*Thus named for the remains of a woman unearthed
from a Rath on The Curragh of Kildare. She died having
been buried alive – a human sacrifice.*

Daghda : Celtic God of the Earth

Shaving

The morning music man
says it's seven-o-four
as I watch your routine ritual
through the half-open door
of the bathroom.

It takes five minutes exactly
as you matter-of-factly
soap the dark shadow
on cheek and chin
and sometimes you tunelessly sing,
gurning your face
into hideous grimaces,
erasing stubble
from awkward places.

Then, oh the seductive
odour of eau de cologne
and I wait for your moan
as the morning music man
says it's seven-twenty –
you've got to go
and I am left
on a zephyr of scent.

The New Man in Naas Post Office

There has to be a woman
behind the bluewhite shirt;
screaming it is, without a word,
of attention above and beyond;

Ava Gardner singing, 'Just My Bill',
in Showboat couldn't have
put it better.

There has to be a woman
behind that green, silk tie
strewn with yellow buttercups,
knotted under his chin
like in my father's time.
The other clerk wears his
like a primed noose.

There has to be a woman
behind that glorious smile,
nervous, a bit apprehensive,
for his first day on display.
Madam, he calls me,
carefully tearing off my stamp
with unaccustomed fingers;

his brand new wedding ring
twinkling under the fluorescent lights.

Sixteen

She's going to the disco
in her best mini-dress,
an outsize sweater,
her hair a mess,
legs encased
in thick white socks
over crimson tights
and Doc Martens.

And she'll dance
the night away
without a care,
better than Ginger Rogers
and Fred Astaire.

What's more
she'll be comfortable
and her feet
won't get sore.

The Day Before the Results

She sleeps peacefully
late into the morning;
I let her, knowing that
she won't sleep at all tonight
for someone somewhere
is sealing a brown envelope
containing the rest of her life.

Figures on a slip of paper
will rest unperturbed
in some Post Office sorting box
until first delivery
in the early morning light.

Then
the gathering, the waiting
of so many sparrows, chirping
in the old school yard
until one by one they are fed
a single crumb.

Will it be a joyful mouthful
or lip-biting disappointment?
Fears and tears
for better or worse?

It's the day before the results.
She's sleeping.
Sh...h...h...h.

Dead Right

I wouldn't be seen dead in that, she said,
though I did my best to entice her
'cause she'd only worn it twice,
but no way was she having my advice.

She said, *That sweater's all wrong*
though the colour's bright,
perhaps I could put it right,
and she reached for my best scissors.

I stopped to amaze
as before my gaze
she cut it full of holes.
Right, she said, *now it's great*,
and she went off on her date.

Did you see that?
I asked the cat,
I wouldn't be seen dead in that.

Thermodynamics

When the door slammed
and you had left –
your angry footsteps
faded into the vast chasm
between us –
mathematical theorems
were the last thing on my mind
as I sat there drooping to sub zero.

Hours later,
when I had totted up
things in my head,
subtracted
your strays from
my hairbrush,
totalled the damp
towels on the floor
and muttered, *good riddance*,
I peeled back your 13.5 tog duvet
only to find your indent insulated,
still warm to my touch.

A mega joule of thermal energy
shocked me out of my standing.

Silver Earring

I know that I will find it
just as soon as I can
pluck up the courage
to enter the empty room,
see the unslept-in bed
and note the perfection
of the unwrinkled counterpane.

Then the residue of your perfume
will sting my eyes to tears
and I will be drawn in
to the realm of nostalgia.

I am not ready for that.

There's something in my throat
that hurts so much
when I think about you.
And when you telephone,
I'll be telling you the truth
when I say that I have not
found your silver earring;
omitting the fact that
I cannot look for it, just yet.

Lesson

He dipped in
his big toe
and said,
I dunno
if I care
very much
for this.

He squinted
one eye
asking,
Must I
get in
and learn
to swim?

Discombobulated

It came from inside his head.
Woke up, he did, he said,
with it rolling off his tongue,
didn't know where he heard it
but he vomited it on the breakfast table,
this word of six syllables
– discombobulated.

Somebody, somewhere,
enunciated it in his presence
and left it hanging in mid-air
to slide into the bytes and RAM
of his open memory
and it was saved there for eternity
– discombobulated.

You might say it disconcerted us
as we could not find it
in our pocket dictionary.
We had to consult the Big Oxford
in the uptown library.
Eureka!
There it was between
discolour and discomfit
– discombobulated.

Optimistic

He stood on a rock
too close to the slushing sea.

I sat and shivered.

He cast and cast
with a fisherman's optimism.

I sat and shivered.

He caught and snared
hook and bait, but retied and waited.

I sat and shivered.

I prayed a mother's prayer that some
suicidal herring would surrender.

I sat and shivered

and practised what face to put on
when he cried out,

Hey Mom, I've caught one!

Gift Horse

He looks at me with big blue eyes
and says,
I have to buy a present
for someone.

My money box is empty
and I have to have
at least
five twenty
for something.

It's very nice
and badly needed,
a surprise
for someone special
on her birthday.

So I count it out,
the exact amount
and wonder –
how long more
must I buy
my own birthday present?

Bad Boys

The demolition squad was here,
I heard the noise outside,
as three claw hammers,
grasped by small hands,
took car after car
from toybox and shed
and shattered them to pieces
with intense determination.

I counted the damage
in Punts and pence
to one hundred pounds
worth of precious Dinkies,
flattened to bits
in our back yard;
because destruction
was the name
of the day's play.

Artefact

Strange
the things you unearth
in the garden.

No archaeologist
could be more awed.

One dinky,
perfect, no rust,
red and yellow
conjuring the picture
of a small boy
in a striped sweater,
a cloth nappy
bulging his blue shorts
in the sunshiny garden.

Humming tunelessly,
I am planting a border
of salvias and something,
while he pulls wriggling worms
from the loosened earth,
forgetting his toy.

He's fifteen now
and with sceptical eyebrow
swears he never
did wear a nappy,
but he wants the Dinky.
It's worth money now.

Treasure

Between the dirt and dust
a bread crust,
a small wheel,
a piece of steel,
a nail,
a pencil,
a miniature machine gun,
a chunk of chewed bubblegum,
the school-milk form
all scruffy and torn,
a football card,
a dried up worm
and in a matchbox
three new pence
and four dead ants,

all fell from his pants
on washday.

Parting

Autumn fluttered between us
as I turned to wave.

You were in the open doorway,
excitement dancing in your eyes.

I drove off quickly and you closed the door
of the place you now call home.

Thomond Bridge is Closed

Miles away from Limerick,
I hear traffic on the Ennis Road
is backed up to Caherdavin.
At the eastern end,
Corbally is busy too
and I follow every line on the road
towards the ancient city walls.

Elbows on my kitchen table,
I cross O'Dwyer Bridge
down into Athlunkard Street,
loving the damp smell
of the Abbey River.

Was that a kingfisher
sniping from the Sally Grove?
And see, see that stream of elver,
inches wide, wriggling homewards
along the river bank, all the way
in from the Sargasso Sea.

On the radio this morning
Roadwatch reports
to the world and its mother,
that Thomond Bridge is closed.
A goose walks over my grave.
The new Ring Road is on the march
and little homes along the Sandmall,
Sheep Street and The Abbey,
must bow to the power of progress.

Saturday Lunch Times

Whist! My father is singing, a steaming mug
of strong tea on the table before him.
In his right hand, a thick slice of Tubridy's
black-crusted cottagebread, smothered with
blackberry jam. His left conducts the radio music:
'Twas down by the Glenside I met an old woman.'

–*Whist*! Mam snaps, *eat your food:* 'A plucking
young nettles, She ne'er saw me coming'. *Whist*!
The neighbours will think you're drunk. I listened a
while to the song she was singing. *That's Arthur
Guinness singing*, she says, with a sigh. 'Glory O,
Glory O to the Bold Fenian men'.
Then she smiles, shakes her head and joins in:
'*Tis fifty long years since I saw the moon beaming*' –
Whist! Now sometimes I hear them on a summer
breeze: 'Glory O, Glory O'. That's my cue to join in
with Leo Maguire's closing lines and Walton's last
word is – *if you feel like singing do sing an Irish song.*
Whist!

September Sunday

Leaving The Parish by Mathew Bridge
I sleech along Georgian Limerick –
Rutland Street, Patrick Street,
up to the Crescent
where well-brassed doctors' doors
wear striped suncoats.

On the hill of O'Connell Avenue,
Micheál O'Hehir tumbles out open windows,
his unique commentary echoing
in the Sunday quiet
to bring armchair fans
the All-Ireland Hurling Final.

And that voice follows me all the way
to Laurel Hill where my knock
on the daunting door of the Reparation Convent
is answered *Deo Gracias* by a contemplative nun
who leads me down through creaking corridors
to the uncomfortable silence of the library.

There, another white sister
chooses my reading matter for me
and I am released to make my way
downtown home to The Parish
with Ben Hur under my arm
Micheál O'Hehir ringing in my head.

* St Mary's Parish, Limerick city, commonly called 'The Parish'

Driving into History

Across the fastforward Slaney,
I follow given directions,
straight onwards,
a right takes me up
the narrow hill,
a left at the church
takes me into a maze of houses
and I bump over ramps
of Fr. Murphy Park.
The final right puts me
in place and there it is –

St. Senan's National School,
Templeshannon,
Vinegar Hill.
High above Enniscorthy,
turf smoke in my nostrils,
I pause to measure
the ancientness of a place
where holy monks once tolled a bell,
where heroes set the heather blazing
down the road at Boolavogue.

This is a seat of learning
o'er the pleasant Slaney
where uniformed children
grapple with the Rs
and emerge under Wexford skies
to take their places
amongst the nations of the Earth,
confident Irish citizens.

Leaving Dingle

Never a one for breakfast,
I steal away,
with great difficulty
controlling the goodbye pangs
until I break through the *draíocht* barrier
winding down Bunbeg Hill.

Coming into Annascaul,
I witness the village
stirring itself to a hoar of ice-blue frost
that leads right up
to the door of The South Pole Inn.

My resolve weakens again at Camp
and tears threaten on the incline
all the way to the top, where I would stop
to drink-in Tralee Bay
but the urge of turning back to Dingle
is so huge I don't dally.

On the flat again
I think of last night's *Coirm Cheoil*,
I can also allow myself to release a tear
to soothe away the awful goodbye ache.
I can allow but I cannot forget
my great romance with the sea
and other things, including
the warm welcome on such a cold night
but that nostalgia provokes a stream
of missing-you-already feelings.

So I pick up this man
with his thumb upturned,
a risky but welcome distraction,
a magpie chattering non-stop nonsense,
his every second word
an impressive, expressive, expletive
in a glorious Kerry brogue.
He is going to Tralee for 'a jar'
trusting his thumb for his going
and homecoming.
He is my diversion.

He breaks the *Daingean Uí Chuise* spell
and I crack a rueful smile
now beyond its magic net,
yet, a voice in my head
keeps calling to me –
Fill, a ghrá, i gceann tamailín.

* *draíocht:* magic
* *Coirm Cheoil: a concert*
* *Daingean Uí Chuise:* Irish name for Dingle town
* *Fill, a ghrá, i gceann tamailín:* Come back again
  soon, love

Oileánach

Always searching for *draíocht*
in the harsh environment,
aware, more than most,
the strange quirks of nature
and a host of *piseogaí*
that mainlanders overlook.

Sé ár ndúchas.
Our heritage.

We see the *sí gaoithe,*
heed its warning,
no one puts out
on water those days.
In the night
we listen for the *olagón*
of the *Maighdean Mhara,*
a cry that comes up
from beneath curled waves,
rolls through the land
to shiver the rocks.

Every swell of the sea,
every mood of the land,
every change in the clouds,
every hue in the sky,
every wave of the wind,
each one a sign to us, to me,
Oileánach.

* *draíocht:* magic * *piseogaí:* a curse / superstitions
* *sí gaoithe:* the fairy breeze
* *Sé ár nduchas:* it is our heritage
* *olagón:* mourning cry
* *Maighdean Mhara:* Mermaid * *Oileánach:* islander

Konopiste

Up through the sloping woods,
a fairy-tale castle on the hill,
all towers and turrets,
glorious in its innocent whiteness,
once home to Austrian Archduke Ferdinand.

Inside, death stalks the walls,
all the way through
corridors and salons,
the trophied heads of forest wildlife
executed for amusement.

A library of notebooks tallies the kills,
big and small, in meticulous hand,
his highly ornate shotguns
displayed in glass cases –
all useless now, the harm done.

The war to end all wars began
when this nobleman, pictured here,
in this fairytale castle with his wife and family,
days before his blue blood stained crimson,
the steps of the cathedral at Sarajevo.

Dachau

Frame i:
There is no need to reach for a camera,
the images will forever
be imprinted on your mind
like black and white negatives.

Frame ii:
Standing under the entrance gate
Arbeit Macht Frei –
Work Makes You Free.
Move on, crunching the gravel
leading to the camp's vast Appellplatz,
the empty Assembly Square.
Picture an awesome silence
assaulting your ears.

Frame iii:
The polished prison corridor,
where each door and footstep
clangs with fearsome authority,
you do not want to be there
but you must focus on the awfulness.

Frame iv:
Outside under the birch trees
a pretty young guide recounts
such horror that makes you turn away
only to be confronted by poplars
planted back then by the persecuted.
Those trees, silent sentinels,
line the Lagerstraße.

Suddenly a stiff breeze rattles
their leaves clattering them
like the dry bones cast into
cavernous ovens on your left there.

Terezin

Sweet-scented lindens, stout and strong,
lead you up the garden path
to this dread fortress of Bohemia.
On the right, behind those trees,
tombstones record the thousands who died;
no, were annihilated,
within these menacing red brick walls.

Through the arched gateway, a courtyard
is confined by administration blocks;
and farther in, cells open into other cells,
each increasingly more terrible,
where every scratch on stone, every mark
on stark wooden benches scream the agony
of those innocents once incarcerated here.

Visitors whisper in a self-inflicted hush,
the putrid dankness seeping into each voice.
Gruesome is the word on the tip of each tongue,
as the guide, proudly wearing his yarmulke,
hammers each horror home in monosyllables
until you can take no more
and leave by the gate bearing this proclamation
Arbeit Macht Frei – Work Makes You Free.

Canadian Spring

I can still hear your voice
from that Spring, reading aloud
across Ontario, in the pickup,
your accent not quite Yankee
but the smoother tones of maple syrup
– Margaret Atwood it was,
satirical, clever, almost inane,
just enough to warrant
an exclamation mark.

Snow in April,
glass forests in the bush,
a beaver slushing between ice floes,
in the tumbling Rogue river,
turkey vultures flocking atop hibernating birch
eyeing the road-kills –
racoon, snake and one bloodied snow goose.

So many trucks rolling too fast,
east and westwards, while we bide our time,
noting signposts to villages
with Highland names
all the way to Lake Huron,
where its crested waves
are but lines of washed-up ice
waiting to melt away,
forgotten in summer sunshine.

But not you, not that spring,
and all those first times on the road to Sarnia.

Famine Burial Ground

Amid Tipperary hills,
a place tilled by the hungry,
fed by their death
in a time when each day
fresh graves yawned
to enfold victims
of tyranny and greed.

Ochone. Ochone.

Here foxgloves shiver
their purple bells,
a lone blackbird
warbles a dirge
above the brown stream,
quiet in prayer
for each blessed release
from a decaying land.

Ochone. Ochone.

* *Ochone:* old Irish lament cry

Fifth of November, 1987

Remember. Remember.

The evening paper says
Roy Rogers,
cool, clean hero is 75.

And someone stole my knickers off the line.

Lester Pigott is 52,
celebrating behind bars,
whilst kidnappers run amok in Dublin.
John O'Grady is alive,
with a mutilated hand,
his fingers boxed in Carlow Cathedral.

Eamonn Andrews died last night.
The dollar
is at an all-time low

and the full moon spotlights my naked line.

Euphoria

When I come down from the ceiling
I'll be fine, I think, but things
will never be the same again.
Perhaps they will or won't. Who's to say?
It's today and I'm on the ceiling.
That's the way I'm feeling.

For so long I was so low,
reaching for long ladders
but those adders had me slithering
farther down into an abyss.

But not today. *No way José.*
Right now I'm on the ceiling.
That's the way I'm feeling.

Please, don't ask me to come off it.

Mae Leonard is originally from Limerick, now living in Co.Kildare. She is a member of Poetry Ireland's Writers in Schools programme. For many years she has been broadcast regularly on RTE Radio One's, *Sunday Misscellany* programme.

Awards include the *Gerard Manley Hopkins Poetry Award*, *Cecil Day-Lewis Award* (for Poetry and Prose), *Scottish International Poetry Awards*, *The Golden Pen*, *Francis MacManus Short Story Competition* and the *Belmont Prize for Children's Poetry*.

Also available from DOGHOUSE:

Heart of Kerry – an anthology of writing
from performers at Poet's Corner, Harty's Bar, Tralee 1992-
2003

Song of the Midnight Fox – Eileen Sheehan

Loose Head & Other Stories – Tommy Frank O'Connor

Both Sides Now - Peter Keane

Shadows Bloom / Scáthanna Faoi Bhláth – haiku by John
W. Sexton, translations, Gabriel Rosenstock

FINGERPRINTS (On Canvas) – Karen O'Connor

Vortex – John W. Sexton

Apples In Winter – Liam Aungier

The Waiting Room – Margaret Galvin

I Met a Man... Gabriel Rosenstock

The DOGHOUSE book of Ballad Poems

The Moon's Daughter – Marion Moynihan

Whales off the Coast of my Bed – Margaret O'Shea

PULSE – Writings on Sliabh Luachra – Tommy Frank
O'Connor

A Bone in my Throat – Catherine Ann Cullen

Morning at Mount Ring – Anatoly Kudryavitsky

Lifetimes – Folklore from Kerry

Kairos – Barbara Smith

Planting a Mouth – Hugh O'Donnell

Down the Sunlit Hall – Eileen Sheehan

New Room Windows – Gréagóir Ó Dúill

Slipping Letters Beneath the Sea – Joseph Horgan

Canals of Memory – Áine Moynihan

pto

Arthur O'Leary & Arthur Sullivan – Musical Journeys from Kerry to the Heart of Victorian England - Bob Fitzsimons

Crossroads – Folklore from Kerry

Real Imaginings – a Kerry anthology, edited by Tommy Frank O'Connor

Touching Stones – Liam Ryan

Where the Music Comes From – Pat Galvin

No Place Like It – Hugh O'Donnell

The Moon Canoe – Jerome Kiely

Via Crucis - David Butler

Capering Moons – Anatoly Kudryavitsky

Notes Towards a Love Song – Aidan Hayes

Watching Clouds – Gerry Boland

Between the Lines – Karen O'Connor

Meeting Mona Lisa – Tommy Frank O'Connor

Every DOGHOUSE book costs €12, postage free, to anywhere in the world (& other known planets). Cheques, Postal Orders (or any legal method) payable to DOGHOUSE, also PAYPAL (www.paypal.com) to doghousepaypal@eircom.net

"Buy a full set of DOGHOUSE books, in time they will be collectors' items" - Gabriel Fitzmaurice, April 12, 2005. DOGHOUSE

P.O. Box 312
Tralee G.P.O.
Tralee
Co. Kerry
Ireland
tel + 353 6671 37547
email doghouse312@eircom.net
www.doghousebooks.ie